# PROVIDENC₁

# PROVIDENCE II

## BY IAN STEPHEN

*Windfall*

PROVIDENCE II was published
with financial assistance from —

• The Western Isles, Skye and
Lochalsh LEADER Group
• Callanish UK Ltd
(Special thanks to Chris Corden)
• Scottish Natural Heritage

The Publisher acknowledges
subsidy from the Scottish Arts
Council towards the publication
of this volume

Graphic design & typesetting by
The Windfall Press

Colour separation & printing by
Nevisprint Ltd, Fort William,
Inverness–shire, PH33 7PQ

**PROVIDENCE II**
**ISBN 1 874167 01 X**
The Windfall Press
Hedmark, 42 Gress
Isle of Lewis, PA86 0NB
Fax 0851–820714

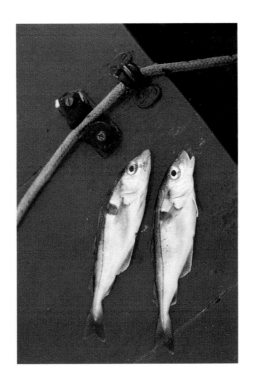

*All royalties from this edition
have been donated to
Friends Of The Earth*

# Contents

# Foreword

*I* grew up in number 66 Kennedy Terrace, Stornoway. This was and is a pebble–dashed house, part of a row which must have parallels in Islands other than Lewis and Harris. We could not look out to sea but it was never very far away. Stornoway was a herring port. I would be sent to the corner shop to buy a score, a measure which was one of many laid out on the back cover of our school jotters. Down the harbour I'd be given half a score, which was one for every digit I could hold out. The fry was taken from the crans, still in the hold after the night fishing. We could go back to the Terraces with hands in gills, held out before. We would leave behind, drying on the concrete, the 'cuddies' which were small fry of lythe, saithe, cod and whiting. Later, I learned that the cuddy was strictly only the young of the saithe or coalfish and in other parts of Scotland the word meant 'horse' but I hold to the meaning the word had in Kennedy Terrace. These fish had gone for a sliver of hand-torn bait, offered on a halfpenny hook to brown cotton line. When you had a bite, you pulled so the fish made an arc through the air to finish against the weeded concrete.

One of our neighbours was on the 'Girl Norma'. She trawled. Nehrops – also known as Dublin Bay prawns – were beginning to be worth something. Airfreight and improved refrigeration made it possible for these to be exported to sit pretty on the top of the paella. A boiling of prawns did not come our way so often. We used to sit up like wee vultures after my father was called, after hours, to open up the Lipton's shop he managed, for a vessel needing provisioned. He would be given a bucketful of the pink shellfish by way of compensation. My mother would do them right away and we would sit cracking and eating them until they were all gone.

Then we'd sleep. We didn't know that the lobster and prawn, the high–status shellfish which boil to red, are the scavengers of the sea–floor. They tear and eat dead things.

We would hear the maroons when the lifeboat went out. Everybody would talk about it. I remember when a small vessel – probably a creel boat called 'Mamie' – was lost. Someone in our street would sing a song about it. It was in English, which was the language of our scheme, except when parents and relatives and neighbours wanted to talk about something you weren't supposed to hear. But it sounded like the Gaelic songs we were taught in school.

And the tone was that of the 78rpm records with the Gaelfon label, played, coveted and lent among the ex-tended family. 'The Mamie' was composed by a woman from the village in South Lochs where the boat was from. The word was that the skipper had been impatient and sailed with a bad forecast. The boat had grounded on the Sgeir Mhor, off The Battery, in the Approaches to Storno-way. The skipper had been impatient again, leaping from his vessel, trying to get onto the reef. The lifeboat saved the others.

Later, I went sea–fishing. Just in time to catch a few of the last of the jumbo haddock and whiting, shoaling either side of the Arnish light. You didn't pull up if you felt only one. They came circling up with the remnants of the raw orange mussel or the white feather lure clear against the grey mouth. Small but plentiful conger and ling survived on reefs

which couldn't be trawled. You could account for twelve species of fish, all colours in the box.

I used to bail the Sea–Angling Club boats and painted them once or twice. As a student with time in my favour – I couldn't read for all the vacations; couldn't afford to travel for all of them and managed with the minimum amount of paid work – I bought a basic plywood catamaran which someone had built from plans. I re–sealed its joints, sanded, primed and painted it with a deep green enamel.

My sea-angling mate got a place on a trawler. Worked his way through his tickets. He got his own thirty-odd footer with colour–sounder, radar, the lot. There's talk of the lenders repossessing it. My other mate, who had just gone through the sail–training part of his Merchant Navy cadet-ship, taught me the basics of sailing on the Spartan but fast cat. I got confident. I cartwheeled it. I remember saying, 'It's OK, it won't go over.'

A boat was lowered from amongst the whitewood barrels lining the decks of one of the Norwegian klondykers, filling–up with solid silver, at Number One pier. The crew helped recover my craft and its floating spars.

I had a couple more years out of the cat on a fresh-water loch on the West Side. It was a way to get out on your own and equally a vehicle to intimacy when a pal or a visitor would share the squat space and work the jib sheets. This was an antidote to pages of notes and library hours. Then I got trapped in the footnotes again. I neglected the cat for a winter, spring and summer. When I returned to the island the catamaran was beyond it. Even on the inland loch, it was unsafe. I burned the wreck.

My father was happy to become sleeping–partner in 'Broad Bay'. She was moored in Stornoway Harbour and named after the shape of sea on the north side of the Eye Peninsula. For some time I'd been taken with all eighteen feet of her line. The Orkney yole has a distinctive deep hull which makes a good sailing shape. I knew to beware of fresh paint but I didn't quite realise that you also had to watch out for bits that feel too hard, unyielding to the tip of your knife. I could cope with repairing the soft bits but was unaware that the stem and stern posts as well as too many of the fat sawn–ribs, were held together by car–body filler.

Her history was written and spoken. I was shocked to find a handwritten entry in the Fishery Office — 'Broad Bay' SY594, Durness, 1912. I did some phoning. An Auxiliary coastguard wrote me to say that Angus and Anson Mackay built yoles at Ardnarkie, Loch Eriboll, for Lewis customers who sailed them home. She spent all her working life setting long–lines out from Coll, Broad Bay.

Yarns came as you worked on the hull, beached at Goat Island shore. The old fellows who re-membered sailing open boats, pow-ered by a lugsail, told you the same things and you couldn't hear them often enough —

*You never tie a sheet. You have to be able to let it go. Don't scrimp on the ballast. Sandbags or rounded boulders and plenty of them so she's more stiff on the reach and better to*

windward. You can always ditch them if you get a heavy haul of fish. Put the reef in sooner rather than later — you won't go faster if you have to spill wind and it's easier to let it go if the wind eases than to lose way, putting it in, if the wind freshens. And you don't run with the wind up your arse. You take it on a quarter. That way you won't gybe. If the wind backs your dipping lug, you're in trouble.

Your mast has lost its only support because that halyard, hardened by a tackle, is secured on your weather gunnel. The weight in your sail is all on your lee side. So you can see you need someone who knows what he's doing on the halyard as well as on the tiller. There are times when that sail has to come down fast and smooth.

What I've done over a dozen or so years is not so much renovation as keeping her on the go. I've spent more time with larch and copper, on the shore, than I've had sailing or jigging for herring or handlining for the smaller haddock which are left. Rediscovering the landmarks I was shown as a kid. Other people have shown me how to make a template for a plank or a sawn frame. They've cut timber for me. Done the jobs which scare me. But I now find myself risking more of these. Bent frames are easy, with a kettle sitting on a driftwood fire and a length of rubber tubing to steam the strips of long–grained oak. These can alternate with the heavier frames and floors. Planks are a matter of nerve, once you've ground through all the fastenings of the old one and transferred the line and bevel of the upper edge. You can justify cheating with marine ply for the artful stern shape of one of the top few strakes of a Stroma Yole[†] like 'Broad Bay'.

[†] Yawl... originallly referred to hull type... In the north of Scotland the term 'yawl' indicates that a boat is yole shape, that is double–ended, with hollow garboards, more or less deadrise, flared sides and raked ends. The Scots yawl is exemplified by the Stroma Yole, which is fuller bodied and higher sided than the Fair Isle or Shetland yoles.
(From *Working Boats of Britain* by Eric McKee
Conway Maritime Press, London 1983)

At first, I sought treated hemp for the running rigging. It looked the part but you never knew how strong it was. Scrounged blocks sometimes did not run sweetly. Once I gybed and the main sheet jammed. By keeping the tiller hard over she came into the wind after dipping a gunnel and swamping. Now I use a type of nylon with acceptable aesthetics and am not afraid to make single–handed life more easy with stainless snap shackles and swivelling Tufnol blocks.

Afloat, after all that work and more, you can see that most things end up in the marine side of the environment. The drifted and wind–bleached plastic bottles along the Atlantic coasts of Lewis and Harris. The diesel film in Stornoway harbour or the more sinister sheen glimpsed in the wake of a chemical–tanker.

I make my living as a Coastguard officer, organising maritime Search and Rescue. More to do with Information Technology than with cliff–rescue lines, these days — but it's still more to me than a job which feeds my family. I don't have to get afloat if conditions are dicey, but if you get to sea now and again, there's a better chance of empathy.

So you read between the logged lines of VHF dialogue—
'Everything all right with you skipper?'
'Aye, aye. No, no problem. Nothing at all. Everything's OK, just thought I'd better give you a shout. There's a bit of sea running out here. Quite a bit like.'

# Providence II

*Venture Fear Not Providence II*
*The first glass is frayed.*

*Moraldie is now a White Rose.*
*The red the green, purple.*

*Astra Forgiveness Diana II*
*Gloss weeps rust.*

*On the Shiant banks*
*colour is translated.*

*Cod pout*
*between the decimals.*

*The Wave Crest is on the slip.*
*Larch lettering is touched.*

# Last Picture Show

We dived from the davits
which floated steel in air.
Rusting rivets on a bedrock.

The lifeboat's buoyancy
went untested.
We were spectacular

with a jack-knife style
or a slow swallow wing.
We shared our harbour

with restless sea-trout
and beer cans on the drift.
We came out clean.

Later the oil had little to do
with the high rig at Glumaig.
Accumulated diesel

crept over our skins
put a scum on our shore
and stopped us swimming.

# Windfall

(for Thomas Matheson)


*That's what she was like, a ghràidh,*
*falling off the wind,*
*falling into it,*
*going like gravity.*

*Thomas, always in the gansey,*
*neighbour over slats,*
*grew worms in his garden.*
*Once a hunter, a ghràidh. But*
*unafraid of endearments.*

*He watched the bubblefloat,*
*as regulator. He was*
*a depressed piston*
*up to strike seatrout*
*somewhere we shouldn't be.*
*If we get results, a ghràidh,*
*we might think about permits.*

*He said to my father,*
*I'll drain your bank a ghràidh,*
*so you can wear carpet–slippers.*
*But my father's eyes were red*
*from the backshop of Lipton's*
*so he paid the coalman*
*and watched the football.*

You couldn't fire a drifter on peat,
a ghràidh, but maybe
there was power in bunks and bootsoles,
falling low on a lee–shore.

I was cook, collier, coiler, a ghràidh.
The hemp was heavy.
We usually found herring.
We couldn't always sell them.

And navigation, a ghràidh.
I got to know the transits
but on the compass and noon–sites
they'd have gone over The Pond
if they'd thought the shoals were thicker.

But the 'Windfall', a ghràidh,
they beached her with the 'Exchequer'.
All the oak accounted for,
holding up high–tensile
to chart the crofts at Ceos.

# Scotch The Diver

*Dave said that Scotch said the seals*
*nudge, take a pull at a flipper*
*while he gropes along a harboured hull.*

*He knows when he nears*
*fouled sterngear*
*as his fellow shapes*
*escalate*
*by placing themselves*
*between the daft one with the tanks*
*and the loom of the ship.*

# Impurities

*I'm tapping on and on*
*at copper points*
*until they burr*
*to retaining domes.*

*Knowing that this shine*
*will get verdigris*
*but glad of the coming*
*impurities of shade*

*and speaking out loud*
*for red tempered green.*

# Boat Burning

*In terms of light it's the longest day.*
*Oyster–catchers are even crazier than*
*ever or since the last time I was here*

*by dried out marine–ply*
*shedding greens and greys. Skelfs*
*breaking free from primers.*

*I strain to see more than*
*what's visible in tones*
*that lie between the*

*timber block moving into*
*charcoal. Loud colour*
*in a stench of flame.*

# Splice

He'd had enough of onshore circuits.
Studied bearings for a ticket.
Fished, mended, steered. Only once

saw a body let go by sea.
Strange things surfaced in the cod–end.
A mine or the carcass of a heifer.

Catriona going for tea and loaf.
Fingers taking up our spikes.
Order of strands and tucks of line.

Tension the splice back on itself.
Risk suited him more than routine.
That's what it came to, net gain.

# Annual
# Maintenance

*It seems to nearly matter what the wind is doing*
*across the tidal mess I've learned to live with.*
*There is an intimation of*
*a backing wind which carries sleet.*

*Some have no option — other than boxes*
*on cluttered forms for the self–employed —*
*but to put to sea with unspectacular resolve*
*and gamble with the fuel–bill.*

*The costs are certain, against*
*what's dragged along*
*a Decca roundabout*
*and power–blocked up.*

*Saleable tails*
*broken from*
*luminous spines.*

*I've still a sort of choice*
*and a lot of buckshee expert help*
*for the problems of my ribs:*
*cut true from a snug template*
*placed on the lap of planks*
*or bent hot from oak straps*
*steamed to tendons.*

# Variables

*Roddy's boat is a Faroes yole
— nineteen foot that won't
go metric. Matt and resin
moulded to pine lines,*

*taking , bow–on, a filling swell
that rises like cumulus.*

*Its silvered engine shakes its
bracket with a steadier
temperament than the
petrol–paraffin combination job
which usually got us far enough to
drop soft mussel
to whiting mouths.*

*Yes, there's healing out here
in the recurrence of variable
conditions. Even though
the sponsons of
St Brendan's boat
bumped bits of oil,
crude and clotted.*

# Hard–Hats

Our lives survived the three months
of fraying fingertips,
stopping against advance of wet.

As the work lulled,
mastic enticed to seams;
roves with an intact shine

held timber in a swelling.
She was down to her gunnels
of undercoated grey.

Her oily glosses
dispelled questions
one Saturday afternoon.

She made her hull–speed
in an electric manner
with the outboard idle.

*A community joined*
*within eighteen feet,*
*dipped the lug, each tack.*

*Under our woollen heads*
*we pretended hard–hats*
*as we beat for harbour*

*and it was a bobsleigh*
*skelping swell*
*taking in small water.*

*It's only now*
*with her bow uphill*
*in drifting shingle*

*and carrying only*
*a specified workload,*
*we allow doubts.*

# Mirror

*The flesh of the Mirror*
*blisters through sheen*

*laminates buckle*
*and International paint*

*falls pale as salmon*
*to the concrete deck.*

# On Ulva

The cattle are Jerseys.
The landowning lady likes
cream on her berries.

A sea–trout net sank
with mullet to silt in
an eddy of Ulva Sound.

Chanterelles fanned
from the black dross.
Vanessa and Kieren

taught me to trust
orange textures.

# Under Beinn Na Drobha

*It's bait–gathering on half–tide.*
*I scour the rocks at Sober Island*
*and remember a rusty Spaniard*

*tied up at Number One. Crew swimming*
*across. Back aboard with black shells.*
*We gave mackerel for bags of wine.*

*Home then in the smell of sour red.*
*The harbour floated*
*a lubricant sheen but*

*we were keen to gut, boil, eat*
*whitefish caught off Sgeir Mhor*
*downtide from the outfall pipe.*

*Now I wouldn't eat fish or bivalve*
*caught in Approaches to Stornoway*
*but my waste goes to Beinn na Drobha*

*the site hidden from the sea,*
*nestled behind landmarks I need*
*and out of mind like domestic debris*

*or these shifting security–cans,*
*drowned or buried in wet or dry*
*insensitive areas .*

# War Memorial

*The word was sacriligeous,*
*apparent as dug–in script*
*on the granite Gaelic cross.*

*The thought word came from years*
*of circles of paper poppies.*
*A collective troop up the hill*
*to spiral by the brass plaques.*

*In this rattling squall of*
*force in whining gusts we*
*hold in the clenching doorway*
*and lip finds familiar lip*
*under the navigation mark .*

*The trench dead and ship drowned*
*would not grudge us*
*our high vantage,*
*in the open.*

# HMS Vanguard

Steel in a primed state
is trollied out,
revealed as seamless.

Imagery is watertight
but the shape will house
a reactor or two
and there are apertures
for death by systems.

The bogey has rolled
too far to cancel:
material is milled
for a fourth one like this

but couldn't we call them
matt samplers
of stitched metals.
Cloth ensigns only
obscuring skills.

*Put on show, as–is,*
*the hull is sculpture,*
*less expensive than opera,*
*in a stretch of history.*

*I wouldn't want it beaten*
*to a sea–plough*
*that scale*
*and sharp enough*
*to sheer scallops*

*but see it as a*
*recumbent memorial.*
*Berthed on a dry plinth.*

# Canoeist

Canoeist, paddle me out
of the backwash here in
the back room made rustic.

Save us from the Friday night heroes
playing Bannockburn and Prince Charlie.
The group in the corner are ready to sing

the full Flower of Scotland.
No–one bothers The Wild Rover no more.
Let's go before Wild Mountain Thyme.

I'm drunk with all the meetings
in this veneered lounge. Bless the guy
who asked me if I was still a runner.

But Iain C on the sway,
skinnier in an outdoor shirt
saying his father still had the drift–net

leaded and corked and the herring
were out there off Tabhaidh Mhor.
We named the crew, wait for weather.

Canoeist come with us. It's not
escaping so long as we know
we're doing nothing so big.

# Chicken Rock

*The panic jig of the first saithe*
*sensed on the handline braid*
*is doubled and redoubled as*

*they pulse in green against*
*the dangling swivel*
*the trailing lead.*

*Our foresail is backed, the boom*
*slides across. Can't anchor here.*
*That's the handbrake.*

*Watch your gear now.*
*We're on the hard ground.*
*Then the dive of a lythe.*

*You are slow in*
*assigning*
*breathing fish to the box.*

*It's not feasible*
*to still*
*each small struggle.*

*Maroon blood on*
*the grey of*
*a thwart.*

# The Bo

*There's still a ling to be had on the bo.*
*You're on the mark when that skyline stone*
*is opening, the war–memorial held.*

*Grunting gurnard and beady–eyed conger are*
*scarce as religious haddock which*
*shoaled over lugworm mud, pectorals swaying.*

*But there's still a colony of ling on*
*this bo which ruins trawls and takes*
*hooks and anchors into its kelp.*

*Our plummeting small–line has broken sea*
*and pulls down the paid–out sequence*
*of spade–end hooks on snoods, softer*

*to touch than brown main line.*
*Sinking cuts of bait sacrificed*
*from belly and iridescent shoulder*

*of mackerel going tense.*
*The lively swivel. The end–stop weight*
*to blue line to marker, pink and daft.*

*Ling with cod–marblings and barbel*
*but an elongated fullness*
*to take a better market price*

*on West–coast floors than all save*
*for lemons, turbot and monks.*
*We're not asking for a box*

*but one to eat when the mooring's found.*
*One for Kenny who gave us the deck–paint.*
*One for Audy who took dry lines down.*

# Recreation

I'm gasping at the gills with fish
swimming in beer and vinegar.
Men, you say, even modern ones
are a disgrace when they're pissed
on rum and heavy and reminiscence.
I want to loiter by bollards and other
signs of what was only recreation —
going to sea in an angling boat with
geared reels made in Reading or Japan.

There's more than crystal sediment
holding to a double bloodknot
that's got as little to do with any club
as it has with kilos of catches.
This unsteady sort of love for
those who saw me as an apprentice
is as reliable as your steadiness
steering me up the road home
and we're not, you say,
setting any alarm
for any morning tide.

# Farewell To Nigg

I left her there above the Spring–mark
with her keel up to meet the hail
but the sprung plank needing something.

You could say I'm near as useless,
hugging stoves and standing at the bars
while my tools are rusting in the box.

We got our start with the welding torch
breathing fire in the pipes at Nigg.
Sleeping on a grounded liner.

Waking up to the twelve–hour shifts
with the sparks sticking in the throat.
So we drank and we sentimentalised.

It was all going to the bank–account,
dreaming boats, crofts and custom cars
but the jobs slid down the firth.

It was fine to see that tall rig we made
gliding out to take the North Sea swell
but home now to signing–on.

With her keel up above the tide,
the light gaping through her hull
she's spilling something from her line.

# Narrative Of Catherine Letreguilly

*1. Stornoway: Conversation after sailing*

*From Sofia to Ankara and Ramadan.*
*Women cooked for us but they couldn't taste it.*

*In the mountains they don't know yet*
*that tourist are for making money.*

*We made harvest. What do you call the fruits of the vine?*
*Too many people for great friendship.*

*We start a strike because the organisers don't work.*
*Is this communism? we say for hours till they work too.*

*Two guys from the Soviet Union are coming.*
*It turns out they don't like much to talk.*

*A guy from Poland drinks two litres of wine.*
*We wake to see him do gymnastics.*

*In the town we see demonstrations.*
*It takes a month to save for shoes —*

*you have the money but no coupons or maybe*
*money and coupons but no shoes in the shops.*

*Now I want to go to Shetland, Iceland, Greenland*
*maybe Canada. I write cards to say OK.*

*2. From Iceland*

*I write to you from your sister's house in Iceland.*
*From Orkney I went to Scrabster then to Faroes.*

*It's difficult to write the sadness when*
*I leave the friends I meet on my way*

*the happiness when I meet the new.*
*I hope you and your father are OK.*


*3. From Greenland*

*I found a boat from Reykjavik to Greenland.*
*This address in Godthaab is 'till September.*


*4. From Boston*

*From Boston I tell you more of my story.*
*I hitch to Reykjavik. Talk to a hundred persons.*

*At the pilot–station they say there's the 'Maelifell'.*
*Thirteen days later I take this ship.*

*A community with radar and satellite navigation.*
*They show me how to work it. We arrive at a mine.*

*I wait in the mess of the mine for the Disko boat.*
*There is no road. I go to the Capital.*

*I arrive at 7 o' clock on Saturday morning.*
*At 8 o' clock I am working in the fish factory.*

*I meet many French people with boats in the harbour.*
*I live aboard one until we have a crew.*

*'Orthersvag' has half–sail half–motor.*
*We take watches south across the Davis Strait.*

*From twelve to six in the afternoon.*
*From midnight to six in the morning.*

*The first night is bad. Icebergs on big seas.*
*But after that is alright for five days.*

*We arrive in Port Manvers.*
*It's not a town just the name of a place.*

*We cook sausages and potatoes on a fire.*
*The first settlers are happy to be on ground.*

*We sail to Nairn and meet Kenny.*
*All his life in the forest. To feed his children*

*he catches animals. Cuts his wood by hand*
*to warm his house and smoke his catch of fish.*

*In Fox harbour we meet a helicopter driver.*
*We cook pizza. He gives me a teddy bear.*

*I take Dave in my Rucksack to Labrador.*
*We meet Jenny and Aggie, singers of country rock.*

*I leave the boat in Port Aux Basques. In Montreal*
*I get a visa for the States from where I write.*

*5. From Oregon*

*I forgot to explain to you the sail*
*between Godthaab and Port Manvers.*

*We hunt for fish and birds on the sea for meat.*
*We see whales sleeping on the sea.*

*One of these has a look to know what is*
*this strange fish which disturbs their quiet.*

*They go down. We sail in ice and fog.*
*We nearly touch icebergs. We hear the noise of ice.*

*Now it's difficult. Always the work–permit.*
*I hope you'll understand my letter.*

# Rackwick Bay

*A place where sound is dominant.*
*Deep breakings from the edge of*
*poor visibility are bound to gather*
*until a slow gasp among the boulders —*
*every one a Brancusi at least,*
*glistening or dry — a multitude*
*from a parable. Subdued signals of*
*catchings and commerce, seagoing ties:*
*fraying strands of synthetic line*
*going to suit the pink in contours.*

*All this visual force is driven by*
*the bay's width of sea. They say*
*it takes seven hours to settle*
*after a gale of wind dies.*

*Your boots are inert and your laces fade*
*like all other lines. The only movement*
*on this shore is in folds and veins.*

*A moaning boom sounds out to all*
*from lingering breeze in cliff caves.*
*A power of light penetrates haar*
*while someone, under a fore–cuddy,*
*fishes the drift off St John's Head.*

*We're surely not the first to need to lie*
*heavily here, open to*
*the dominance of sound*
*and slower sympathetic sense.*

# Sugar Loaf Island Farallons, 1868–69

(from a photograph by Carleton E. Watkins)

*This chunk, suffering a long exposure*
*before and after Carleton shipped his gear.*

*Baked and crusted to show fissures.*
*Higher reaches iced in guano.*

*Smooth and lower random rocks*
*can't stay still, reveal themselves as*

*sea–lions stretching the limits*
*of salt and silver.*

# Return To Lochinver

So this is the place stamped wood boxes
should be returned to. Thursday
is the big market night.

Soyea and its proximate skerries
are breaking seas out
under a sea fog which survives

the southwesterly 5.
The first position we got
for the 'Loch Erisort'

was inside that island,
fixed by pyrotechnic red
reported on the 999.

We pencilled on the charts.
VHF unreadable.
Lochinver lifeboat took one,

the fishery–cruiser another.
Colours of clothing were passed.
The SeaKing arrived but the rest

was up to the divers and the telex.
Carriage–returns and shifting spaces.
Paperwork and logging for the Inquiry.

# On The Coast
# Of Fife

*The crack of sycamore.*
*The two biting firths.*

*When we grow warm we talk*
*of Polar–maritime movements.*

*The jack sailed from Whitby*
*with a writ on his mast:*

*a transit to Faroes.*
*Crazy Wayfarers to Iceland.*

*Icelanders clearing Barra Head,*
*not believing the crashing glass.*

*A Canadian canoe off Calgary, Mull,*
*seal squadrons sniffing its paddling.*

*Linda singing to steer the child queen*
*from Bergen to Burntisland.*

*Our sleeping–bags let loose,*
*carried by groundswell.*

# Red Sail

*Fred Iverson, your red sail*
*is no symbol.*
*It's bent with hemp*
*to a salted spar,*
*an encrusted cringle.*

*Primary dye has absences —*
*cirrus traces, bleached–in.*
*The thing is romantic enough*
*without further mention.*

*Sent on its traveller*
*up the linseed sheen*
*to set its own high peak*
*against what's over us*
*and just out of stretch*
*of our tight halyard.*

# Red Lead

*My present standpoint makes way.*
*Able seamen stab at rust.*
*I'll go for specific orange,*
*locally in its place as*
*a temporary stop*
*of singing oxide.*

*I bide within limited parallels.*
*Shuffle a few meridians.*
*Too much point or too much span*
*fail to fix a position.*

*Elegies are all about.*
*I'm for red lead.*
*A brush with poison*
*startling against decay.*

# Resolve

*A steadying staysail.
The transmission
under the mizzen.
Imploding cylinders
maintain compression.*

# *Transit Bearing*

*I'm not talking*
*tidal diamonds*
*written pretty by*
*the magenta finger*
*of God or the Hydrographer.*

*Take the rock that's the sail,*
*white with creases*
*of whin yellow,*
*needle green.*
*Open on Gob a' Chuilg.*
*Now on your quarter.*
*Keep them.*

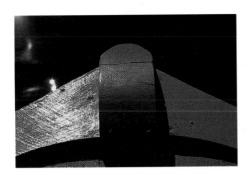

# Haiku

*mesh is let down deep*
*under metres of green veins*
*herring come alive*

*three navigators*
*as resolute halibut*
*white bellies swimming.*

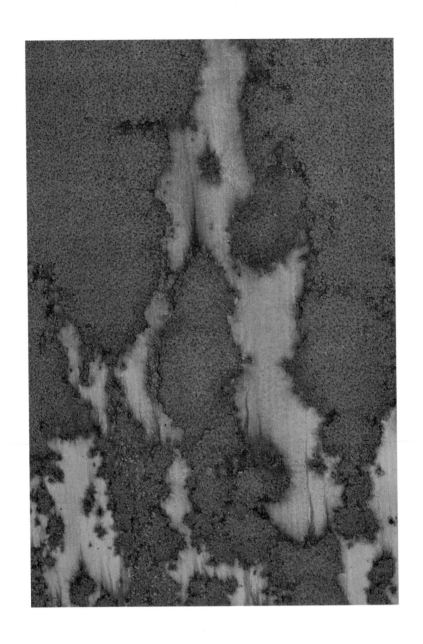

# Pigment

*pigment and oil and wood*
*sympathise*
*bleach to skies above*

*reds seep out*
*pale*
*to dulse below*

# Broad Bay

*These primed patches express*
*metallic pink, blotched blues,*
*rounding at their edges.*

*These clinker boards are crossed*
*by retaining courlene*
*orange lines*
*to Goat Island.*

*Timbers are of differing soundness.*
*Bitumen seeps to dry bilges.*
*Planed grain shows.*

*Wind tan on exposed skins.*
*Traces of compounds*
*may or may not*
*preserve us.*

# Orain Luaidh

*Tweed and silk
are on the table.*

*We trawl our cloth
to trap the mackerel.*

*Seas and skies
rusty as crotal.*

*Our arms sent out
in a free–for–all.*

*Trimming sails
on waves of maple.*

# Layers

*Red is feasible in*
*the first layer of sea*
*under near lap of scales.*

*The pelagic ones dive*
*through pink to krill*
*which glint yellow*
*at the unsaturated*

*edge of green merging*
*into the demersal*
*province of blue.*

# At Mudeford

At Mudeford, rigs rattle
stainless shrouds.
Alloy shine salted matt.

Ken says the beamers here
have dragged–out the damage
pursers did West and North.

The same crushing reasons —
fishermen netted by overheads
so bruising all down below.

Ken's hands, like his son's,
are widened out like dough.
Have little left to prove.

# *Raku*

*K*azugo, *Shuntaro*, *Gozo*:
*I didn't know you.*
*Our words from random drifts*
*met as stranded timbers*
*piled with elements of control*
*above a tidal level.*

*Riddling of round bits of stone*
*and the whisper of*
*cormorants going by.*

*Raku smoke*
*made the Coigeach blink.*

# Coigeach To Stac Pollaidh

We like to think we delve
deep, with our spiky talk,
not scared of bone,
a complex break
from stag or ewe
gone green as the bog it's in
— the seepage from the Coigeach
collecting in cultivations
by the headland fort
now fallen wild.

And up eroding steps
to that exposed spine
broken through as summits
from the cold exhaust.
A shock–load of skyline.

I stole sense of live shapes:
the clink of their protection.
Someone quoted 'western buttress'
to define their route.

I couldn't see Stac Pollaidh
as any bit of castle
so huddled, open–ended
as a karabiner
before the gate is home.

# Boatbuilder —
# Scoraig Peninsula

Christopher Dawson build your boats,
the one on the stocks and the sketched.
They can take a historical shape
or are jigged on wind–driven gear
from fresh–sawn templates.

You build the larch arks,
patent–steamed, frequently–fastened
and I'll patch the larch relic
I took responsibility for.
Trying not to have ourselves on
as we sign our subscriptions —
small coupons on born–again paper.

Tonight it is obscene to be obsessed
with shape shown in words or wood.
Missiles are anti somebody, somewhere
Our kids will wake at their own time.
We'll refill beakers, dab at sore bits,
counter old and new in our shapes,
trusting that horror will not flood
those who huddle in land–borne walls.

# East Coast

1. From Banff to Aberdeen

High bows rose from Banff to Aberdeen,
whale–backed to take the acres
of newly delivered trap.
So the silver went to folding money.
Daimlers waited, rusting on quays.
Skippers bought horses for dry daughters.
Herring, mackerel, ground to meal
to plump poultry and pigs.
Vessels for sale now
in The Fishing News.

2. At Rosehearty

I crouched and never more so.
Smelled the easterly gale.
Sensed the North Sea weight
from this stone–walled stance.
A lean hard fathom of bolster
causing the unstoppable to break
around its own limits
in clean spittle and fume.

Knowing, never more so, its
spacious constellation gleam,
diverse from the slow rasp
of shag–green spurdog skin
to a single stickleback dart
with fifteen spines on its back.

# Markets

*Pick–ups back to hooked boxes*
*in The Broch and Peterheid.*
*The progression of Doric price*
*over the purr of Caterpillars,*
*the remembered Kelvin.*

*The stamping, hot breath and*
*bids taking me along to*
*the auction pens at*
*Kennedy Terrace and*
*the look my uncle gave when I said,*
*full of Primary Geography,*
*the beasts had gaps in their sides*
*like the maps of the Moray Firth.*

# Reach

On a beam reach, the belly
of the hull takes knocks.
You have to trust
the keel that's under you.

Broadening the reach,
a longer, relaxing lope
follows confused butting.
Destabilises.

# I'll Boil The Kettle

*I'll boil the kettle since the mainlight's on,*
*breaking areas of angle–poise arcs*
*on colour–coded panels of contacts.*

*The skipper of the 'Golden Sheaf' can*
*pass the tow by radio–telephone:*
*'Over to you, Calum, at Loch Sealg.*
*The bacon and eggs are on, below*
*and I'd better see about getting a crust*
*to share between the boys on Friday.'*

*That tone is set against the residue*
*of another task, a further latitude,*
*clear of the Butt and at eight degrees west.*
*A crewman simply went over the rails.*
*He jumped out to the calm night.*
*They threw fluorescence, lowered a boat.*

*We sent a chopper with potent spans*
*of live lights. It found only*
*lit buoys and flotation as*
*a brash litany of failed hopes.*

# *Bracelet*

*A bracelet of small stuff*
*failed to support him.*
*The frayed fibre strands*

*teased out*
*in orange and blue*
*on a yellow cuff,*

*adhering and asking*
*if these fastenings*
*were desperate*

*before the wind–chill*
*and ingested spray*
*came inside him.*

*Or were working–lashings*
*against seep of damp*
*from all directions*

*fixed before the crises*
*that must have begun*
*like any small snag,*

*the three strands biting*
*the sweating steel*
*of the running hauler?*

*Or was cordage knotted*
*as she went over*
*so the suit might float*

*or the body be secured*
*to the hull that swamped?*
*But two were lost*

*and only returned*
*with weed and small stuff*
*when tides relented.*

# Turron De Alemandra Blando

(loss of the "Frank C", October 1991)

*Pounded almonds are recognisable*
*in oil and honey, binding*
*this rich residue.*

*I have to return to the foil.*
*No–one else here likes*
*the soluble salt sweet.*

*A present from a trawler's owner.*
*From Bilbao to The Rockall Trough.*
*Machinery failed and she floundered*

*with her sidewinders ports*
*open as mouths to the swells*
*and no–one shouting the distress.*

*The survivor's narrative*
*tumbled in rubber*
*through plotted patterns of drift.*

*Sorties of searches from Stornoway,*
*Cornwall, Kinross, Keflavik.*
*White water walls. Blotted screens.*

*All our trawls yielded only thanks,*
*diplomacy and brandy;*
*almond plankton.*

# Night Watch

*The slant of the night watch*
*is away from the obvious.*
*Audible burr presides.*

*The 'Girl Lauren' calls.*
*Dodging off the Kebock.*
*It's a poor night.*
*It's the clutch.*
*If we get her jammed in gear*
*we'll go for Ullapool.*

*No, no, not making much of it.*
*Most likely make for Stornoway.*
*It's a very poor night now.*

*The cream barograph settles low*
*so tide is bumped above tables.*
*The 'Suilven' floats open–mouthed*
*above the linkspan.*
*Police close the isthmus.*

*At Branahuie, stranded drivers*
*blink at the appearance*
*of the Shiants.*
*This time the sea goes back.*
*Shed tails of kelp are left*
*on the asphalt.*

# In The Harris Hotel

John Munro, in the hotel bar,
was placid about lifesaving:
the lugging of hawsers which
took on water before
they entered it
and got strained
by the dogged–on tackle,
shore to ship and spitting
more than orders by numbers.

But the ones who screeched
at local eddies and
took the knife to gear and
couldn't find a budget for a battery
to search the night
were full of shit.

That was all and there wasn't
much point in being smart
about these things.

# At The Herring

*At the herring this year,*
*in the September dips*
*between a protractor span*
*of rays to near dark:*
*the sky of skate wings*
*in black butter —*

*pilots navigate past*
*The Chicken and*
*white–beaked dolphins*
*jump like late salmon*
*which also swim by.*

# Leading Light

There was fire round the boat today.
Visible hot frost on a thwart
to singe my own distrusts.

Quiet, under daylight phosphor.
Spring–rate setting
slack tan line away.

Blatant white without the usual red
in a plotted descent — no help
towards degrees of steering.

I throttle up spark in the carb
to chase emanations from
leading intuition of the bow.

# Tangles

*Tangles wrap rock*
*fade but*
*insinuate*
*glaring pattern.*

# Stranding

*They would have been a wave–fall*
*of flesh and oil but now*
*wide livers are chased through*
*for metals and reasons.*

# Razorfishing (Low Water Springs)

*The main implements are prints of boots*
*spaced by a trusting backwards walk.*
*You have to look for the shellfish show.*
*It's no good when it's behind you.*

*Salt red nicks take hold of you*
*and are dismissed,*
*the blending tints of bleeding*
*aside like the gloves,*
*shed in the hotting–up*
*of this cold harvest*
*that's a bit of a hunt.*

*There is a transference*
*of skills like spores*
*passed quietly*
*in the flexible*
*medium of sand.*

# Drifting

*Anchored in the cocked–hat intersection*
*of bearings to conspicuous headlands,*
*I'm drifting outside intentions*
*while firm in a familiar place,*
*hooking a named species of fish.*

*A sensitive row of hyphens along*
*the lateral line: glimmer of radar.*
*The smouldering flush*
*failing in foreign air.*

*Soundings to close*
*or distant concerns.*
*Caesium is carried*
*on the indecisive tide*
*Mines are moored*
*or cast–off.*

*Insistent geography*
*as thoughts go*
*their own way*
*in slack water.*

# The Stuff Is Squeezed

*The stuff is squeezed*
*under rock waves*
*and amassing seas.*

*Released and routed*
*to a holding chamber,*
*black liquid bones*

*suspended in*
*a hull husk*
*and moved.*

*Ships slide the gaps.*
*Eilean Trodday to Comet Rock.*
*Gob Rubha Uisenis to*

*the quick green light*
*northwest of the outlying fins,*
*the lazy cetaceans*

*of backlit stone — the*
*extended islands, the*
*family of Shiants.*

*Or westabout with the long*
*fetch of prevailing seas*
*a dull ache on your beam.*

*And when it gets to where it's going,*
*narrowed and sent out again, I feed*
*it to my moist cylinders,*

*give it air and fire and know*
*that hydrocarbons leak.*

# Losgaintir

*The form of your foot fits*
*in a swamped crater.*
*You grow from flecked white*
*of Traigh Losgaintir.*

*Your salt–clogged hair*
*is rippled like*
*long abrasions*
*in sea sand.*

*I take you all in*
*and trust that threats,*
*overhead or undersea,*
*will remain remote*

*or be quietened*
*like the hard blue lines*
*grown hairy in*
*this range of tides.*

# Sound Of Harris

(for Ivor Horton, Surveyor and Coastguard)

Here, the tides talk in Norse
and flood in conjunction
with prevailing spindrift.
You do not see the gradient of waters,
only the shoulders of fiords:
Loch A Ghlinne, Resort, Tamnavay.

To the south, set is composed
of midstreams and side–issues.
The flood takes–off on a beam reach
to scour by Coppay, bounce Ensay,
nudging from Rhenish to the Uists
in a contrary cycle.

Even the cartographer concedes
special treatment for the Sound Of Harris
and orientates the latitude scale
across the vellum.
You navigate
in diagonals.

# Bothy —
# Taransay Island

(for Ewan Macrae, Creelfisher and Ferryman)

*It had a sort of dead quality —*
*when he beached here before, in Uidhe Bay.*
*A place quiet because the people left.*

*Maybe it was the refurbished gables*
*that offended him or the sharp roof*
*before he even saw the Meccano system*

*of T and A pieces to take bolts*
*in live joists and rafters. Or maybe*
*he didn't like the scent of creosote*

*stealing downwind from the shelter.*
*It could have been the direct nylon red*
*of socks drying on Taransay stone.*

*If I was trying to go back,*
*pushed by six horses of the Suzuki,*
*I'd rather go further than the ruins*

*and cramped hints of cultivation.*
*There were five souls in 1961,*
*descended from rumoured hundreds.*

*After his spiel I need to know*
*from archives more adequately housed,*
*what they sowed and what evicted them.*

# Southwest Harris

*This island is discontent as light*
*glanced under precipitation:*
*a weather system from south of Islay.*
*Ireland is there, under Malin Head.*

*A melting landmass in the dunes of*
*Seilebost. Toe–Head out as an arm*
*but insufficient to shield the machair.*
*Then there are katabatic bursts of wind*
*against the grain of decent predictions*
*bringing destroying light*
*from Clisham and Mullach bho–dheas,*
*brushing deep below the surfaces*
*of the Sound of Taransay,*
*bringing only change.*

# Under Roinebhal

A tense lattice of radio mast
opens over the square spire of
a church with a galley, in stone.

Flexing fins on
the starting flood.

Kelp cod falls on
cotton delft smock.

We lure lythe under Roinebhal,
a mountain to be shipped
for hard white infill.

Maybe we'll lose
only our bearings.

# Running For Home

*I'd rather take that white at the bow*
*when the sea is making like a burn.*
*Following you, surf intimidates.*
*Your quarter is always one plank low.*
*You trust the iron's not going sick.*

*Haddock spill to bottom boards.*
*They're seared with thumbprints*
*bare to air on paler greys.*
*Saturated colour in the bait —*
*mussel strands adhering to the lips.*

*We don't always get the other's name*
*and could be less evasive in*
*the exchange of marks.*
*You'll also wear a proud groove*
*from terylene twitch on the index finger.*
*And I'm right glad to be coming home*
*in the tail of your wake tonight.*

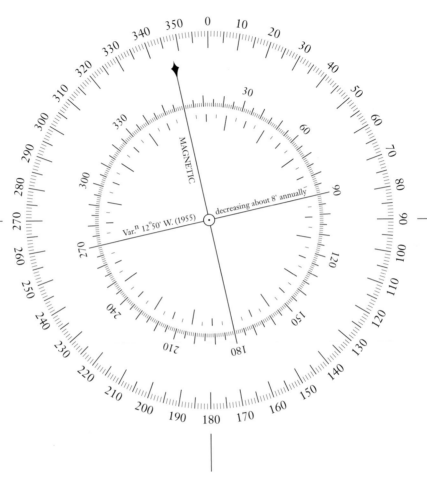

MAGNETIC

Var.ⁿ 12°50' W. (1955)   decreasing about 8' annually

# Guide Me

*Guide Me Ocean Gift Bride Of Tolsta*
*Muirneag on Diobadail*
*Paraffinn varnish*
*Muirneag on Tiumpan*
*Roved in iron*
*Just so much give*
*The breasts on Tabhaidh*
*Diligence Venture*
*Sawn frames and steam bent*
*The grey house open*
*Arnish on Holm*

*The spar on the Beasts*
*Lilac Daffodil*
*The three second sector*
*Galilean*
*Blinking from Stoneyfield*
*Phosphor bronze thrust plate*
*Abeam Goat Island*
*Two fixed greens*
*Peace And Plenty*

# Biography

Ian Stephen was born in Stornoway in 1955. He graduated from Aberdeen University, and now works as a Coastguard Officer on the Isle of Lewis. His poetry and short stories have been published in several countries including Australia, Belgium, Canada, Denmark, Ireland, Switzerland, United States. He is also a storyteller and has collaborated with artists and musicians, including Sean O' Rourke, Savourna Stevenson, Alasdair Fraser, Dick Gaughan, The Keltz.

Three poems from *Malin, Hebrides, Minches* were set to music by Diethelm Zuckmantel and performed in Dusseldorf in 1992.

His photographic work has been published in *The Scotsman*, *Scotland on Sunday*, and publications by Acair, Stornoway. He has presented a programme on *Poetry and Landscape* at the A.A. School of Architecture, London.

Much of this book is based on two exhibitions originated by *An Lanntair*, Stornoway. Versions of these poems have appeared in the following publications —
*Chapman, Gairfish, Gown, Hjok Finnie's Sanglines, Kunapipi, Northlight, Northwords, Resurgence, Strata, The West Highland Free Press, Buoyage — A Morning Star Folio.*

# Previous Publications

| | |
|---|---|
| *Malin, Hebrides, Minches* | Dangaroo Press, Denmark 1983 |
| *Poems for BZ* | Poetry Australia, Berrima 1987 |
| *Varying States of Grace* | Polygon, Edinburgh 1989 |
| *Siud an t–Eilean* (Editor) | Acair, Stornoway 1993 |
| *Buoyage*<br>(A Folio with Will Maclean) | Morning Star, Edinburgh 1993 |
| *A Semblance Of Steering*<br>(With Will Maclean) | Morning Star, Edinburgh 1994 |